The Olive Tree

The Mystery of the Church and Israel

Randall Rittenberry

Emphasis within scripture quotations is the author's own.

The Olive Tree

The Mystery of Israel and the Church

ISBN: 979-8-9887417-3-2

Printed in the United States of America

Compass Publishing
USA

TABLE OF CONTENTS

Preface 5

Chapter One: Promise and Covenant 9

Chapter Two: Jacob, Israel, and Exodus 13

Chapter Three: The Everlasting Covenant 19

Chapter Four: Was Israel Rejected? 23

Chapter Five: Restoration and Repentance 29

Chapter Six: Land Promises 35

Chapter Seven: Not All Israel 41

Chapter Eight: Engraftment Theology 47

Chapter Nine: The Spirit of Antichrist 57

Chapter Ten: Politics and the World 67

Conclusion 75

About the Author 77

Bibliography 79

PREFACE

In the days following the events of October 7th, 2023, when Hamas attacked Israel, there has been a rise in anti-Israel and anti-Jewish sentiment. Shortly after those events, Islamic groups, along with faux social justice groups, began to protest Israel. They were not concerned about the brutality of an unprovoked attack, nor were they concerned about the deaths of Israeli children or the hostages who were taken. No, the narrative almost immediately became one of somehow blaming Israel and justifying that brutal attack against them. Not long after, government officials from around the world began to demand that Israel either not respond or show restraint, for "the Palestinian children," of course. Again, this showed no sympathy for the deaths of Israeli children and adults, nor empathy for the families of those who were murdered or taken hostage. Then, on cue, the media of the world echoed that view. They have gone so far as to blame Israel for the deaths of Palestinian children when Israel struck back, and they have created villains for the world to hate. The reporting has been one-sided, and facts have been withheld as the narrative against Israel continues.

Not long after the protests started, we were told by politicians, activists, and media members that these were just peaceful protests against the government of Israel; we were assured that individual Jews would not be targeted. Again, the narrative did not match reality. Since the war in Gaza broke out, anti-Jewish incidents have risen across the world.[1] In America, we still remember the Jewish students trapped by "peaceful protesters" on the campus of New York University in New York City on October 25th, 2023. The protests escalated to physical threats against Jews, contrary to what we were assured. Look at what has transpired in the days since Hamas attacked Israel.:

- Between October 7th, 2023, and September 2024, there were 10,000 anti-Jew incidents reported.[2]
- These include 1,800 reported acts of vandalism against Jewish institutions and cemeteries, 150 individual assaults, and 1,000 bomb and security threats against Jewish synagogues and schools.[2]
- Over 2,000 incidents specifically targeting Jewish institutions.[2]
- College campuses saw a 500% increase in anti-Jewish incidents, with a reported 1,200 cases.[2]

These incidents are not isolated to the United States. Countries around the world have seen increases in reported incidents.[2] The statistics above represent a 337% increase in reported incidents compared to the year prior to the outbreak of the war in Gaza.[2] In the United Kingdom, 4,103 anti-Jewish incidents were recorded. Of those incidents, 2,699 were reported after October 7th, 2023.[2] This trend has continued into 2025, but complete statistics have not been released as of this writing.[3] What is important to see here is that what starts as protests against the government of Israel quickly devolves into the persecution of Jewish people. The deception being peddled is that criticism of Israel's government is not the same as persecuting the Jewish people. But we see that this is not true. Criticism of Israel's government is simply a smokescreen for the real intent: Jewish persecution and the removal of the nation of Israel from the

Middle East. Remember the chants: "From the river to the sea…." This phrase is a one-sentence summary of intent: the annihilation of Israel not only as a nation-state, but also of those individuals of Israeli descent.

Throughout history, the nation of Israel has been more hated, despised, and lied about than any other nation. We see it throughout history. Although hatred for Israel has always been a fact of history, we are currently seeing an entire world beginning to unify against Israel. We know from Scripture that this was coming and will continue. We expect the world to behave this way. It is prophecy, and it is inevitable. What is most disturbing, however, is the rise in anti-Israel sentiment among people who claim to follow Christ. Believers are joining the cause against Israel and trying to use Scripture to justify it. To be fair, this has been going on in the church since AD 150 with the rise of Justin Martyr's replacement theology, or supersessionism.[4] But it seems to be gaining ground rapidly among believers against the backdrop of the current political climate in the world today. It has not helped that very popular media commentators and social media influencers are promoting this theory through their substantial platforms. Theories and myths regarding Israel are being repeated, just as they were before the Holocaust.

I believe that many people simply want to be on the right side of history and want the atrocities of war to stop, while others are pursuing agendas that fulfill their own personal ambitions. Regardless of intent, the result is cooperation with the spirit of antichrist, which seeks to blind people to its true intent: to destroy the nation and people of Israel and, with that, the destruction of God's promises through His word. The intent of the spirit of antichrist has always been to diminish the power of God and His word in the hearts of people. satan knows that he cannot defeat

God physically, so he introduces Luciferian doctrine and destroys faith in God. The goal is to defeat God by undermining the promises of God. It will not work, but those involved in this game through politics, money, and the pursuit of notoriety are headed off a cliff and are taking precious lives with them.

The purpose of this book is to shed light on what Scripture says about God's promises to Israel, His plan for Israel, and the relationship between Israel and the church. Together, we will look at current thoughts, falsehoods, conspiracies, and myths surrounding past and current events regarding Israel. We will look at both the spiritual and theological view and the worldly and political view. Through this, I hope those aligned against Israel will repent, and those aligned with Israel will be strengthened. Remember what the scriptures say in Psalm 122:6-9: *"Pray for the peace of Jerusalem: May they prosper who love you! Peace be within your walls and security within your towers! For my brothers and companions' sake, I will now say, "Peace be within you." Because of the house of the Lord our God, I will seek your good."*

Chapter One:

Promise and Covenant

Israel! The very mention of this country elicits powerful emotions in people across the world. The amount of emotion and energy expended on this tiny country seems disproportionate to its size. Its capital, Jerusalem, is called the center of the world.[1] There are many influencers, leaders of industry, politicians, media personalities, and celebrities in today's political climate who call into question the existence of Israel as a nation. They claim that the Jewish state is illegitimate. They simultaneously claim that Palestinians are the rightful claimants to that land. Again, so much passion and opinion over such a tiny piece of land. Why? Because, like it or not, believe it or not, the conflict over the land in that part of the world is a spiritual battle.

What should we believe about Israel? Why does it matter? For the believer, what we believe about Israel affects our views on the New Covenant, our views on the end times (eschatology), and influences our faith regarding the nature and character of God.

From a natural perspective, it is hard to believe the impact that tiny plot of land has on the world today. But we are not dealing with the natural. We are dealing with principles, promises, and covenants of supernatural origin that have an eternal purpose. If we are to understand the spiritual significance of the Middle East conflict, we must look to where this all began. It began centuries ago when God called one man to leave his family and his country and travel to a land that the Lord would show him: Abram (later called Abraham). In Genesis 12:1–3, we read: "*Now the Lord said to Abram, 'Go from your country, your family, and your father's house to the land that I will show you. I will make of you a great nation; I will bless you and make your name great, so that you will be a blessing. I will bless them who bless you and curse him who curses you and in you all families of the earth will be blessed.'*"

This marks the beginning of what is known as the "Abrahamic Covenant." There is nothing to indicate why this promise made to Abram thousands of years ago would cause so much conflict through the ages to this day. Then we arrive at Genesis 12:7: "*The Lord appeared to Abram and said, 'To your descendants I will give this land….'*" The conflict comes from the promise of land to Abram's descendants. This is the starting point of the Middle East conflict, ground zero, so to speak.

In the Abrahamic Covenant, the Lord promises to Abram (Abraham): to make him into a great nation (Genesis 12:2), to bless him (Genesis 12:2; 22:17), to make his name great (Genesis 12:2), to be a blessing (Genesis 12:2), to bless those who bless him and curse those who curse him (Genesis 12:3), to bless all the families of the earth through him (Genesis 12:3; 22:18), to give him and his descendants land (Genesis 12:7; 13:15; 15:7; 15:18–21; 17:8), to give him innumerable descendants (Genesis 13:16; 15:5; 22:17), that he would go to his ancestors in peace at a very old age (Genesis 15:15), to make him a father of many nations, and that kings would come from him (Genesis 17:5–6), and that He would multiply his descendants (Genesis 22:17).

The conflict that arises from Genesis 12:7 is that both Jews and Arabs/Muslims claim the promise is for them, as both are descendants of Abraham. The Arab/Muslim world stakes its claim to that land through their ancestor, Ishmael. Ishmael was the son of Abraham, conceived through his wife's servant, Hagar (Genesis 16). It is through that ancestry that the Arab/Muslim world views everything in relation to Israel. Israel stakes its claim through Isaac, the son of Abraham's wife, Sarah (Sarai). But we must ask: does the Abrahamic Covenant include all of Abraham's descendants?

The Child of Promise

For the believer, we must answer this question about the Abrahamic Covenant and Abraham's descendants from the biblical record. What does God's Word say? We find the answer in Genesis 17. Keep in mind that this takes place after Abraham conceives Ishmael with Hagar at Sarah's request (Genesis 16). Also, keep in mind that the context is that Abraham asks God for the covenant to go to Ishmael because of his unbelief that Sarah will conceive a son (Genesis 17:15–18). Genesis 17:19 then says, *"Then God said, 'No, but your wife* ***Sarah*** *will bear you a son, and you will call his name* ***Isaac****. I will* ***establish My covenant with him*** *as an everlasting covenant, and with his descendants after him.'"* The will of God to establish and continue the Abrahamic Covenant is repeated in Genesis 17:21[2], once again in the context of the Lord saying He will bless Ishmael (Genesis 17:20). It is absolutely God's heart that the Abrahamic Covenant belongs to the descendants of Isaac, not Ishmael.

Any claim by Arabs/Muslims through the lineage of Ishmael is not valid from a biblical perspective. Hebrews 11:18 says that God told Abraham, "*...Through Isaac shall your seed be named.*" Why did God choose Isaac instead of Ishmael? We find the answer in Romans 9:11: *"For before the children had been born, having done neither* *evil nor good, so that the purpose of God according to* **election** *might stand,* **not of works,** *but through Him who calls."* Isaac was the son of promise because Ishmael was born of works. Another way to say it is that Ishmael was born of the will of Abraham's flesh, man's will, and not God's. The promise must stand through the election of God; otherwise, it would not be a promise of God, but a work of the flesh through the strength of man. In other words, it would not be of grace.

It is God's covenant that is promised to Abraham and his descendants through Isaac. In Genesis 15, God makes the covenant with Himself (Genesis 15:17–21; Genesis 22:16; Hebrews 6:13–14). It is His faithfulness at stake, as we will see more clearly as we continue. The Lord calls this covenant "My covenant" in Genesis 17:2, 4, 7, 9, 19, and 21. This is important because it shows that this covenant is not based on man's works, but on God's faithfulness. God did not reject Ishmael (Genesis 17:20). He rejected the premise of His covenant being based on man's will and strength. Through God's promise and grace, the Abrahamic Covenant passed to Isaac and his descendants, who would become Israel.

We see the Lord give the same blessing to Isaac in Genesis 26:2–4: *"The Lord appeared to him and said, 'Do not go down to Egypt. Live in the land of which I will tell you. Sojourn in this land, and I will be with you and will bless you; for I will give to you and all your descendants all these lands, and I will fulfill the oath which I swore to Abraham your father. I will make your descendants multiply as the stars of the heavens and will give your descendants all these lands. By your descendants all the nations of the earth will be blessed.'"* This confirms Isaac as the child of promise.

CHAPTER TWO:

JACOB, ISRAEL, AND EXODUS

As we discussed in the previous chapter, the Abrahamic Covenant passed to Abraham's son by Sarah: Isaac. We see in Genesis 25:21–26 that Isaac had twin sons, Jacob and Esau. Esau was born first, so he was the eldest. It was the custom at that time to name the eldest son as heir. Under that tradition, Esau would have inherited the Abrahamic Covenant. The Abrahamic Covenant should have passed to Esau. However, once again, the election of God was the determining factor as to who received the Abrahamic Covenant. The Lord foretold this to Isaac's wife, Rebekah, in Genesis 25:23: *"Then the Lord said to her, 'Two nations are in your womb, and two peoples will be separated from your body; one people will be stronger than the other, and the older will serve the younger.'"* This election was proven true when Esau sold his birthright for soup (Genesis 25:29–34).

Romans 9:10–12 says, *"Not only that, but Rebekah also had conceived by one man, our father Isaac. For before the children had been born, having done neither evil nor good, so that the purpose of God according to* **election** *might stand,* **not of works**, *but through Him who calls, it was said to her, 'The elder shall serve the younger.'"* It is the Lord who established not only this covenant, but also to whom the covenant would be given. Jacob was given the inheritance instead of Esau, even though it went against the traditions of men. What we glean from this for our lives is that, in two instances of the inheritance of the Abrahamic Covenant, neither the will of man nor the traditions of men dictate the purposes of God. It is *"through Him who calls."* That makes it absolute and beyond dispute. Hebrews 6:16-17 plainly states this: *"For men indeed swear by a greater authority than themselves, and for them an oath of confirmation ends all dispute. So God, wanting to show more abundantly the immutability of His counsel to the heirs of promise, confirmed it by an oath."*

Jacob Becomes Israel

Scripture shows the Abrahamic Covenant passing to Jacob in Genesis 28:3–4. In that account, Jacob leaves Canaan and his family to find a wife. As Jacob begins to leave, Isaac says: *"May God Almighty bless you and make you fruitful and multiply you, so that you may become a multitude of people. May He give you* ***the blessing of Abraham****, to you and your descendants with you, that you may inherit the land where you are a stranger, which God gave to Abraham."* This is the Abrahamic Covenant, stated in the same kind of language God used with Abraham and Isaac when conferring it.

In verses 13–14 of the same chapter, we read the Lord speaking to Jacob in a dream: *"I am the Lord God of Abraham your father and the God of Isaac. The land on which you lie, to you will I give it and to your descendants. Your descendants will be like the dust of the earth, and you will spread abroad to the west and to the east and to the north and to the south, and in you and in your descendants all the families of the earth will be blessed."*

This is the same language and promises of the covenant God gave to Abraham. In Genesis 32:28, the Lord renamed Jacob Israel. It is to Jacob (Israel) that the birthright of the Abrahamic Covenant, including the land, is given. This is a major key in understanding where we should place our support as believers. It is ultimately Jacob's descendants who are included in the promises, not Abraham's or Isaac's. Abraham and Isaac had other descendants. We will look at that in another chapter. For now, we will focus on the patriarch on whom the covenant was ultimately conferred. That patriarch was Jacob, or Israel.

From this point forward in Scripture, God does not extend the Abrahamic Covenant to only one man in Abraham's line; He extends it to all of Jacob's sons, collectively known as Israel, which fulfills the promise of blessing to Jacob's descendants. This is how we know where to place our support: Israel is given the promises and the land.

Abraham and The Exodus

Is there another way to identify which of Abraham's descendants received the Abrahamic Covenant? In Genesis 15, we see the Lord initiate and confirm a covenant with Abraham (Abram). Before the Lord walked through the pieces of sacrifice, signifying the cutting of a covenant, He prophesied to Abram in verses 13–14: *"Know for certain that your descendants will live as strangers in a land that is not theirs, and they will be enslaved and mistreated for four hundred years. But I will judge the nation that they serve, and afterward they will come out with great possessions."* This is a prophecy of Israel being slaves in Egypt. The biblical account of how the tribes of Israel came to Egypt begins with Joseph being sold into slavery by his jealous brothers in Genesis 37. We read the account of Joseph in Egypt in Genesis 39–41. Joseph went from slave to second in command in Egypt through God's favor.

A famine came upon the land, but through the wisdom God gave to Joseph, Egypt was well prepared. During the famine, Joseph's brothers came to buy food from Egypt. They did not recognize Joseph, but eventually Joseph revealed himself. The tribes moved to Egypt at Joseph's request (Genesis 42–47). Even during this time, we see God working to save Israel and fulfill His promise to Israel. In Genesis 45, Joseph speaks to his brothers and says in verses 5–8: *"Now do not be upset or angry with yourselves because you sold me here, for God sent me before you to* ***preserve life****. For these two years the famine has been in the land, and there are still five years in which there will be neither plowing nor harvesting. God sent me ahead of you* ***to preserve you*** *as a remnant on the earth* ***and to save your lives*** *by a great deliverance."* God is faithful to His Word and His promises! Eventually, the tribes of Israel became slaves in Egypt, and we pick up that account in Exodus 1.

Exodus 1:8–14 describes what happened after Joseph's death: *"Now there rose up a new king over Egypt, who did not know Joseph. He said to his people, "Surely, the people of the sons of Israel are more numerous and powerful than we. Come, let us deal wisely with them, lest they multiply, and it come to pass that when any war breaks out, they also join our enemies, and fight against us, and escape from the land." Therefore they set taskmasters over them to afflict them with their labor. They built for Pharaoh storage cities: Pithom and Rameses. But the more they afflicted them, the more they multiplied and grew so that as a result they abhorred the sons of Israel. The Egyptians made the children of Israel to serve with rigor, and they made their lives bitter with hard service—in mortar and in brick, and in all manner of service in the field, all their service in which they made them serve was with rigor."* This is exactly what the Lord prophesied to Abraham about his descendants. And the descendants this happened to were the descendants of Jacob's sons: the tribes of Israel!

In Genesis 15, the Lord also told Abraham that He would judge the nation that oppressed these descendants. We see that judgment in Exodus 7–12 through the ten plagues on Egypt. When Israel was finally freed by Pharaoh, Exodus 12:35–36 records this: *"Now the children of Israel did according to the word of Moses, and they requested of the Egyptians* ***articles of silver and articles of gold, and clothing****. And the Lord gave the people favor in the sight of the Egyptians, so that* ***they gave them what they requested. Thus they plundered the Egyptians****."* Again, this happened exactly as the Lord promised Abraham in Genesis 15.

The Exodus account confirms which of Abraham's and Isaac's descendants are heirs to the Abrahamic Covenant, based on what the Lord told Abraham just before the covenant was cut. Jacob (Israel) and his descendants are the rightful heirs of the Abrahamic Covenant, which includes the land defined in that covenant.

CHAPTER THREE:

THE EVERLASTING COVENANT

The Abrahamic Covenant is called an everlasting covenant by the Lord in Genesis 17:7. That means every promise contained within this covenant is promised forever. That includes the promise of the land: physical, literal land. If it were not literal, it would not be listed with boundaries. There are teachings within the body of Christ that claim the land promises are spiritual or allegorical, and that these promises ultimately point to Heaven as our promised land. But that is not the picture we get from Scripture. God establishes boundaries, literal boundaries, and lists the tribes of people living within those boundaries in Genesis 15:18–21. The southern boundaries are mentioned in Exodus 23:31 and Ezekiel 47:19. The western boundaries are mentioned in Numbers 34:7–6 and Ezekiel 47:20. The northern boundaries are listed in Deuteronomy 11:24, Ezekiel 47:17, and Joshua 1:4. The eastern boundaries are listed in Numbers 34:11–12 and Ezekiel 47:18.

There are at least 170 Scriptures that mention the land God promised to Abraham and his descendants. Within those Scriptures, it is stated that God gave them land by an oath fifty-five times.[1] Twelve times it says it is an everlasting promise, or that it is forever.[1] One such Scripture is Isaiah 60:21: *"Then will all Your people be righteous and they will possess the land* ***forever*** *…"* This cannot be taken lightly. We either believe God is faithful, or He is not. If this promise is not literal, then how can we trust that the New Covenant promises are literal? It is intellectually dishonest to pick and choose which promises are literal and which are allegorical. Did Jesus literally come in the flesh? Did Jesus literally die on a cross for our sins? Was Jesus literally resurrected from the dead for our righteousness? Did Jesus literally ascend to the Father in Heaven? Does Jesus literally sit at the right hand of God? Will He literally return to the earth?

As I stated earlier, how we view the Abrahamic Covenant will influence our views on nearly everything else, including the New Covenant. Is God's Word true? Is it plain, or do we have to run it through a deciphering code? I believe many people employ spiritual and allegorical interpretive devices because doing so gives them control over how they want to see things and allows them to justify their biases. The biblical standard is to adjust our view to what Scripture says, not the other way around. A literal interpretation, except where the text clearly indicates symbolism or allegory, is the only way Scripture makes sense. Any other approach causes confusion and can create a form of Gnosticism.[2] Numbers 23:19 says, *"God is not a man, that He should lie, nor a son of man, that He should repent. Has He spoken, and will He not do it? Or has He spoken, and will He not make it good?"* What He says, He means. He has said in multiple places that He gave Abraham and his descendants the land of Canaan, which we know today as Israel. It is an everlasting covenant.

In the New Testament, the author of Hebrews writes concerning the Abrahamic Covenant in Hebrews 6:13–14: *"For when God made a promise to Abraham, because He could vow by no one greater, He vowed by Himself, saying, 'Surely I will bless you, and surely I will multiply you.'"* God made a vow with Himself to keep the promises of the covenant to Abram. It is vitally important that we understand this point. The Lord bound Himself to this promise through the spiritual legalities of the covenant.[3] One way God is sovereign is that He holds Himself to His own laws. He does not lie, nor does He break oaths, as we saw earlier in Numbers 23:19. The Abrahamic Covenant can never be broken. Galatians 3:17–18 bears this out: *"And this I say, that the law, which came four hundred and thirty years later, does not annul the covenant that was ratified by God in Christ, so as to nullify the promise. For if the inheritance comes from the law, it no longer comes from the promise. But God gave it to Abraham through a promise."* In the context of Israel, the Apostle Paul also says in Romans 11:29: *"For the gifts and calling of God are irrevocable (without repentance, KJV)."*

Abraham, Isaac, and Jacob

The Lord promised each of the patriarchs an everlasting covenant. It is promised to Abraham in Genesis 17:7: *"I will establish My covenant between Me and you and your descendants after you throughout their generations for an* ***everlasting*** *covenant, to be God to you and your descendants after you."* He promises that Isaac will inherit an everlasting covenant in Genesis 17:19: *"Then God said, 'No, but your wife Sarah will bear you a son, and you will call his name* ***Isaac****. I will establish My covenant with him as an* ***everlasting*** *covenant and with his descendants after him.'"* The covenant to Jacob and Israel is called everlasting in 1 Chronicles 16:15–17 and Psalm 105:8–10. Both passages say: *"He remembers His covenant forever, the word that He commanded, to a thousand generations, that covenant He made with* ***Abraham****, and His oath to* ***Isaac****, and confirmed to* ***Jacob*** *as a decree, and to* ***Israel*** *for an everlasting* ***covenant****."*

The question to the body of Christ is this: Does God keep His Word?

CHAPTER FOUR:

WAS ISRAEL REJECTED?

One argument used to justify anti-Israel and anti-Jewish sentiment is the contention that Israel has been rejected by God. There are a few Scriptures used to make this claim. One such Scripture is Matthew 23:37–38: *"O Jerusalem, Jerusalem, you who kill the prophets and stone those who are sent to you, how often I would have gathered your children together as a hen gathers her chicks under her wings, but you would not! Look,* ***your house is left to you desolate.****"* Another is Matthew 21:43: *"Therefore I tell you, the kingdom of God* ***will be taken from you*** *and given to a nation bearing its fruits."* Let's take a closer look at these passages and see if Jesus pronounced rejection over Israel. In Matthew 23:37–38 and Matthew 21:43, we must establish context. The context begins in verse 2: *"The* ***scribes and the Pharisees*** *sit in Moses' seat."* Jesus then goes on to explain the burdens that the scribes and Pharisees placed on the Jewish people (verses 3–7). From verses 13–36, Jesus addresses the **scribes and Pharisees**.

Matthew 21:43 is in the context of a parable Jesus spoke that began in verse 33. The gist of the parable is that every time God sent a prophet to Israel, the leaders (priests and kings) killed them. Finally, God sent His Son, and they (the leaders) killed the Son as well. It is in this context that Jesus said the kingdom of God would be taken from them (the priests and leaders). The next-to-last line of that chapter (verse 45) says this: *"When the chief priests and Pharisees heard His parables, they perceived that He was* ***speaking of them****."* Jesus did not pronounce judgment or rejection over the Jews or the nation of Israel. He pronounced rejection and judgment on the **leaders** and the religious system that had been corrupted by those leaders. What Jesus pronounced in Matthew 23:38 was prophetic judgment. That judgment came to pass in AD 70 with the destruction of the temple and Jerusalem by the Romans.

In Hebrews 8:8–12, the author quotes Jeremiah 31:31–34, which is a prophecy of the coming New Covenant. In verse 9, the author declares that the Lord rejected them because they broke the covenant. Does that mean He rejected all of Israel? The context speaks of when the Lord brought Israel out of Egypt. He rejected **that** generation. Indeed, that generation was not allowed to enter the promised land because of their unbelief. The same account is mentioned in Hebrews 3:7–11, which says, *"Therefore I was angry with* ***that generation****, and said, 'They always go astray in their heart, and they have not known My ways. So I swore in My wrath, they* ***shall not enter*** *My rest.'"* What we see is that the Lord will reject certain generations of people, but He will not reject His promise. We have established that He made an everlasting covenant with Abraham, Isaac, and Jacob. We either believe God is faithful, or we do not believe He is faithful. His sovereignty is key. Does His sovereignty allow Him to change His mind about a covenant, or does it bind Him to His word?

Jeremiah 1:12 says, *"The Lord said to me, 'You have seen correctly, for I am watching to see that my word is fulfilled.'"* (NIV) We must also consider Isaiah 55:11: *"So is my word that goes out from my mouth: It will not return to me empty but will accomplish what I desire and achieve the purpose for which I sent it."* This issue is not just about the possible rejection of Israel; it is about the character of God. Sovereignty is not about arbitrary decisions or changing one's mind on a whim. The picture we see in Scripture is that of spiritual law and God holding Himself to His word. In fact, we see this in Ezekiel 36:22, where the Lord said, *"Therefore say to the house of Israel, Thus says the Lord God: I do not do this for your sake, O house of Israel, but for My holy name's sake..."* In other words, God fulfills His promises because His name and word are tied to His character and His sovereignty. What will He do for Israel? We see the context in verse 24: *"For I will take you from among the nations and gather you out of all countries and will* ***bring you into your own land****."*

We see something similar in the New Testament. Interestingly, it is also about the Jews. In Romans 3:1–4, the Apostle Paul says, *"What advantage then does the Jew have? Or what profit is there in circumcision? Much in every way! Chiefly because the oracles of God were entrusted to them. What if some did not believe?* ***Would their unbelief nullify the faithfulness of God?*** *God forbid! Let God be true, and every man a liar..."* God's sovereignty means He keeps His word. When He says a covenant is everlasting, He does not change His mind. Ethnic Jews have not been rejected because the promise has not been rejected. Romans 11:29, speaking of Israel and the Jews, is very clear on this: *"For the gifts and calling of God are irrevocable."* God still has them in His plans. In fact, this Scripture is in the context of the Lord presenting His plan of salvation to Israel once again: Jesus, the Messiah. It is His faithfulness to His word that is the determining factor of the promise.

Divorce and Redemption

A Scripture that is often used to try to prove that the Lord has rejected Israel is Jeremiah 3:8. In that verse, the Lord said He gave

Israel a "bill of divorce." In this verse, He is speaking of the northern kingdom being taken captive by the Assyrians in 722 BC. He is speaking in the context of bringing Judah to repentance to avoid the same fate. Nevertheless, Judah did not fully repent and was taken into Babylonian captivity over a period of several years; the final fall of Jerusalem was in 586 BC. These "divorces" were a direct result of both kingdoms violating the covenant of the Mosaic Law (Psalm 78:10; Isaiah 42:24; Leviticus 26:44).

Regarding Judah (the southern kingdom), their captivity was temporary. Nehemiah returned to finish rebuilding Jerusalem in 444 BC at the behest of Artaxerxes I, and those in captivity were allowed to return if they chose. This was a direct fulfillment of the prophecy in Daniel 9:24–25, which started the prophetic clock known as 'Daniel's 70 weeks'.

The northern kingdom (Israel) did not return from their captivity. But even after mentioning the "bill of divorce" in Jeremiah 3:8, the Lord calls out to them to return to Him in verse 12. Punishment was temporary, based on the temporary nature of the Mosaic Law. But remember, the law did not annul the Abrahamic Covenant (Galatians 3:17–18). The land promises are still in effect. I would argue that we will never see the Jews removed from the land again because of the New Covenant. Hebrews 8:8–12 teaches us that the New Covenant was to the houses of Israel and Judah, and that He would forgive them and remember their sins and iniquities no more. Because of this, there will be an expansion of ALL Israelites in the land (Deuteronomy 30:5). Amos 9:15 is a future prophecy that says, *"I will plant them upon their land, and* **no more** *will they be uprooted out of their land which I have given them.* **The Lord your God** *has spoken."*

Has God rejected Israel? Has He divorced them? Repeatedly, the prophets warned of impending judgment, but they also spoke of restoration and repentance. The primary message of the prophets was redemption. Even during those times of captivity and after the return of Judah (the Jews), the prophets continually prophesied the return of both Israel and Judah to the land by the Spirit of the Lord. Jeremiah 30:3 says, *"For surely the days are coming, says the Lord, when I will restore the fortunes of My people Israel and Judah. The Lord says, I also will cause them to return to the land that I gave to their fathers, and they shall possess it."* Since 1948, the Jews have been returning to Israel. The Jews are the descendants of the three tribes that made up the southern kingdom of Judah after the kingdom of Israel split: Judah, Benjamin, and Levi (the priests).

The prophets, however, distinctly mention both Israel and Judah. So, anytime we see this phrasing, it is speaking of a future fulfillment of those prophecies. If Israel has been divorced and rejected, then why are there so many prophecies about their return? If the Lord does not have plans for them, how do we account for this Scripture in Jeremiah 29:11: *"For I know the plans that I have for you, says the Lord, plans for peace and not for evil, to give you* ***a future and a hope****."* I know we like to use this verse as individuals, and we can because God is no respecter of persons. But the true context of this verse is Jeremiah prophesying to those in Babylonian captivity. Then the Lord, through Jeremiah, says this in verse 14: *"… and I will turn away your captivity and gather you from* ***all the nations and from all the places*** *where I have driven you, says the Lord, and I will bring you back into the place from where I caused you to be carried away captive."*

Notice that this verse says the Lord will *"gather you from all the nations and from all the places."* Judah was only taken to Babylon. Jeremiah is prophesying the return of all Israelites to Israel, not specifically the return of Judah, which began under the Medo-Persian Empire. He would not have used the plurals "nations" and "places" if that were the case. He also said the Lord will *"turn away your captivity."* That did not happen when the Jews returned from Babylon. They did not have autonomous and sovereign rule as a nation. They were subjects of different empires. Autonomy and sovereignty for Jews in Israel did not happen again until 1948. All the prophets point to a future fulfillment because God knows *"the plans I have for* you (Israel)." Furthermore, Jeremiah 31:35–37 makes clear that Israel will never cease to be a nation before the Lord.

Isaiah 40:2 says that Israel received double for all her sins, but that at the appointed time her iniquity will be pardoned. It seems from verse 3 that the appointed time was the coming of the New Covenant.[1] When read in conjunction with Hebrews 8:8–12, we must conclude that God did judge Israel for breaking the covenant (Mosaic Law). God also judged the Judaistic system of the Pharisees and Sadducees in AD 70. Judgment does not equal rejection, although those things are often conflated to justify certain beliefs. God has not rejected His promise to the descendants of Abraham, Isaac, and Jacob. He has forgiven them. He has not rejected the Jews. In Romans 1:1-2, the Apostle Paul says, *"I say then, has God rejected His people? God forbid! For I also am an Israelite, a descendant of Abraham, of the tribe of Benjamin.* ***God has not rejected*** *His people whom He foreknew…."*

Isaiah 14:1 says, *"The Lord will have compassion on Jacob; once again* ***He will choose Israel****…"*

Leviticus 26:44–45 says, *"Yet for all that, when they are in the land of their enemies, I* ***will not cast them away, nor*** *will I abhor them to* ***destroy them*** *utterly and to break My covenant with them, for I am the Lord their God."*

CHAPTER FIVE:

RESTORATION AND REPENTANCE

The return and restoration of Israel are major themes of the biblical prophets. These themes are repeated multiple times in the books of the prophets. The restoration of Israel to the land will be the fulfillment of God's promise to Abraham, Isaac, and Jacob. Romans 11:28 says, *"…but as regarding the **election**, they are beloved for the sake of the **patriarchs**."* This verse is followed by verse 29, which says that *"the gifts and callings of God are irrevocable."* In other words, they do not change. Malachi 3:6 says that the reason Israel *("sons of Jacob")* is not destroyed is because of His unchanging nature. This makes the promise to Abraham's descendants through Isaac and Jacob immutable, unable to be changed. As we have seen previously, it is an everlasting covenant. Time and again through the prophets, the Lord delivered the message of judgment, but ultimately restoration.

It is estimated that there are 365 prophecies concerning the land belonging to the Israelites and their return to the land. Before we look at a few of those, let's look at two New Testament references in the book of Acts. The first is Acts 1:6, just before Jesus' ascension into heaven: *"So when they had come together, they asked Him, 'Lord, will You at this time restore the kingdom to Israel?"* The disciples asked specifically about the restoration of Israel. At the time of this question, the Jews were still in Israel (called Judea by the Romans). However, they were not autonomous or sovereign. At that point in time, the Jewish people considered restoration as a return to the days of King David and King Solomon: a kingdom that was autonomous, and whose land and resources belonged to the nation of Israel. That is the mindset that frames this question to Jesus from the disciples.

Jesus answers their question in Acts 1:7: *"He said to them, 'It is not for you to know the times or the dates, which the Father has fixed by His own authority.'"* This was after the resurrection. He did not correct them or tell them that Israel had lost the kingdom forever, or that it would never return to Israel. No, Jesus said only the Father knows when that would happen. This implies that restoration **will** happen. If not, He would have told them.

Then we see this verse in Acts 3:20–21: *"and that he may send the Messiah, who has been appointed for you—even Jesus. Heaven must receive him until the time comes for God to* ***restore everything****, as he promised long ago through his holy prophets"* (NIV). Peter is preaching to Jews when he mentions a "time of restoring." The King James Version renders this phrase as *"the times of restitution of all things."* What is to be restored? He answers that with *"what God spoke through all His holy prophets."*

In context, Peter was preaching repentance to the Jews as one of the "all things" the prophets spoke about. He even references the Abrahamic Covenant (verse 25). But as we have seen, to the Jewish mind, it meant the restoration of sovereignty and autonomy to Israel, along with a king in the line of David who would rule from Jerusalem. That is how the Jews at that time viewed restoration. There were prophecies concerning this, such as Jeremiah 23:5-6: "*The days are coming, says the Lord, that I will raise up for David a righteous Branch, and he shall reign as king and deal wisely, and shall execute justice and righteousness in the earth. In his days Judah will be saved, and Israel will dwell safely, and this is the name by which he will be called: THE LORD OUR RIGHTEOUSNESS."* This also aligns with end-times prophecies concerning an everlasting kingdom (Daniel 2:34–35; Daniel 7:27; Isaiah 9:6–7).

There are multiple Scriptures from the prophets regarding the restoration of Israel and their return to the land the Lord promised them. This is not the only restoration, but it is one of the "**all** things" that Peter spoke to the Jews. Everything the Lord spoke through the prophets will be restored, as promised. Isaiah 11:11-12 says, *"In that day the Lord shall set His hand again* ***the second time*** *to recover the remnant of His people, who shall be left, from Assyria, from Egypt, from Pathros, from Cush, from Elam, from Shinar, from Hamath, and from the islands of the sea. He shall set up a banner for the nations, and shall assemble the outcasts of Israel, and* ***gather together*** *the dispersed of Judah from the four corners of the earth."* This is a prophecy in the context of the second coming of Jesus (verses 6-9). We see parallels in Matthew 24:31, Mark 13:27, Micah 4:6-7, Isaiah 56:8; Ezekiel 39:28; Deuteronomy 30:3-4, Nehemiah 1:9, Ezekiel 11:17, Ezekiel 20:34 and 41, Ezekiel 28:25, Ezekiel 34:13, Ezekiel 36:24, Ezekiel 37:21, Zechariah 10:10, Isaiah 43:5-6, Jeremiah 31:8, Jeremiah 31:10, and Psalm 147:2-3.

The Repentance of Israel

Israel will be given another visitation and opportunity to accept Jesus as the Messiah during the tribulation (Isaiah 11:11). Scripture teaches that Israel will receive Jesus as their Messiah. We see this most clearly in Zechariah 12:10: *"And I will pour out on the house of David and the inhabitants of Jerusalem a spirit of grace and supplication. They will look on me,* ***the one they have pierced****, and* *they will mourn for him as one mourns for an only child, and grieve bitterly for him as one grieves for a firstborn son."* This is a picture of repentance. We see this in other Scriptures as well. The prophets spoke of a time when the Lord would raise a king like David, or in the line of David. The prophets were speaking of Jesus and His genealogical ties to David. Revelation 19:15 gives us a description of Jesus coming as a warrior king, which is in the likeness of David. Here are some more Scriptures that speak of Israel receiving their King (repentance) and of Him ruling over them: Ezekiel 37:24; Hosea 3:4–5; Jeremiah 23:5–6; and Jeremiah 30:9. All of these events will fulfill the Abrahamic Covenant as well as the Davidic Covenant (2 Samuel 7:12–16). The Lord even promises repentance in Deuteronomy 30:6.

The Effect of Restoration and Repentance

Romans 11:12 and 15 describe the effect that Israel's restoration will have: *"But if their transgression means riches for the world, and their loss means riches for the Gentiles, how much greater riches will their full inclusion bring! For if their rejection brought reconciliation to the world, what will their acceptance be but life from the dead?"* This fulfills the promise to Abraham in Genesis 12:3 and Genesis 22:18, where the Lord says, "and all peoples on earth will be blessed through you."

We see this partially fulfilled through the gospel of the finished work of Jesus being preached to the whole world and through Gentiles being grafted into the kingdom of God (Romans 11:17). However, its ultimate fulfillment will occur when the Lord returns to the earth and Israel turns to its Messiah. Understanding why God will save Israel is important for New Testament believers because it builds hope, which leads to faith being established in our hearts (Hebrews 11:1). If God fulfills promises made thousands of years ago, including those made under the old covenant, how much more will He fulfill the promises made to those who are in Christ? We have a better covenant (Hebrews 8:6).

Chapter Six:

Land Promises

We saw in Chapter 4 that Jesus told the scribes and Pharisees that the kingdom would be taken from them (Matthew 21:43). However, He never said that the Abrahamic Covenant was taken from them, nor the land promises. The Apostle Paul wrote in Romans 9:4: "*who are Israelites, to whom belong the adoption, the glory, the covenants, the giving of the law, the service of God, and the promises.*" These things belong to the Israelites, and this was written **after** the resurrection and **during** the formation of the church. A major part of those covenants was the promise of land, especially the Abrahamic Covenant, which Galatians 3:17 says cannot be annulled. Repeatedly, the Lord promised Abraham, Isaac, Jacob, and their descendants a specific piece of land with defined boundaries. This cannot be interpreted spiritually or allegorically. He also repeatedly promises to bring Israel back into that land. Let us look at some of these Scriptures:

Ezekiel 36:24, 28
"For I will take you from among the nations and gather you out of all countries and will bring you ***into your own land. You will dwell in the land that I gave to your fathers****. And you will be My people, and I will be your God."*

Ezekiel 37:21, 25
"Say to them, Thus says the Lord God: I will take the sons of Israel from among the nations where they have gone and will gather them on every side and bring them **into their own land. They shall dwell in the land that I have given to Jacob** *My servant, in which your fathers lived. And they shall dwell in it, they and their sons and their son's sons forever…."*

Ezekiel 39:28
"Then they will know that I am the Lord their God because I made them go into exile among the nations, and then **gathered them again to their own land;** *and I will leave none of them there any longer."*

Amos 9:15
"I will **plant them upon their land,** *and no more will they be uprooted out of their land which I have given them. The Lord your God has spoken."*

Jeremiah 30:3
"For surely the days are coming, says the Lord, when I will restore the fortunes of My people Israel and Judah. The Lord says, I also will cause them to **return to the land that I gave to their fathers, and they shall possess it.***"*

Zechariah 8:7-8 "Thus says the Lord of Hosts: I will deliver My people from the eastern lands and from the western lands. And I will bring them, and they will reside in Jerusalem, and they will be for Me as a people, and I will be for them as God, with faithfulness and righteousness."

Isaiah 14:1 "For the Lord will have mercy on Jacob, and will yet choose Israel, ***and set them in their own land****."*

Jeremiah 32:37 "See, I will gather them out of all countries wherever I have driven them in My anger, and in My fury, and in great wrath; and I will bring them again to this place, and I will cause them to dwell safely."

What we must understand about these Scriptures is that most of them were written during the Babylonian captivity. The Jews returned from Babylon, so it would seem that these prophecies refer to that return. But there are two things to note: 1) the Lord mentions both Israel and Judah in many restoration Scriptures, or *"my people"*, meaning all of Israel; and 2) many of these prophecies were not completely fulfilled during the return from Babylon. They never had autonomy or sovereignty, they were driven out again by the Romans, and they have not dwelt safely since returning from Babylon or since the establishment of a Jewish state in 1948. That means these prophecies look forward; they have a future fulfillment. We saw the beginning of that fulfillment in 1948. We will see that promise continue to be fulfilled until Jesus returns and restores all things, including the promises of land made under the Abrahamic Covenant.

The Valley of Dry Bones

In Ezekiel 37:1–14, we see a very famous prophecy and vision about a valley full of dry bones. The Lord commands Ezekiel to speak to these bones so they will come alive (verse 4). Ezekiel does as the Lord commands, and the bones come together, along with tendons and skin. This prophecy is often used to encourage people that God will restore their lives, which is fine. But that is not the context or the interpretation. We get the interpretation in verse 11: *"Then He said to me, 'Son of man, these bones are the* ***whole house of Israel****....'"* "Whole house" meaning both kingdoms, Israel and Judah. Verse 14 then records what the Lord says through Ezekiel: *"And I shall put My Spirit in you, and you shall live, and I shall place you* ***in your own land****...."* This verse tells us that when the Lord restores Israel to the land, salvation will also come (*"put my Spirit in you"*; see also Romans 11:26). This prophecy speaks directly to God's plan and desire for Israel.

Immediately after this vision, the Lord gives another prophecy for Israel: the prophecy of the two sticks (verses 15–22). To summarize, on one stick Ezekiel was commanded to write "Judah," and on the other, "Joseph." Ezekiel was to keep them in one hand, and when asked what it meant, he was to say that the Lord would take the two sticks and make them into one stick. Many people have interpreted this to mean the church, in reference to Ephesians 2:15, where the Apostle Paul said Jews and Gentiles would become "one new man." While the *"one new man"* is certainly a true theological principle, this is not what the Lord intends in this prophecy. The *"one new man"* is intended to illustrate the spiritual reality in Christ that all who receive Him are spiritually united in Him; there is no separation or distinction in our spiritual position (Galatians 3:28).* To understand what the Lord is saying in the prophecy of the two sticks, we must look at the context. The context is the restoration of Israel back to the land.

Ezekiel prophesied this during the time of the Babylonian exile. Remember, the united monarchy under King David and King Solomon split into two nations after the death of King Solomon:

the northern and southern kingdoms. The northern kingdom retained the name Israel, and the southern kingdom became Judah, named after the largest of the three tribes that composed that kingdom. Judah returned to the land after the Medo-Persians defeated Babylon; the northern kingdom did not. So, this prophecy is pointing to future fulfillment. It drives home the point that **both** would return one day and unite once again. It is not a prophecy of joining Jews and Gentiles together as one through the church. It is a literal prophecy of restoring and reuniting all of Israel.

The restoration of Israel is twofold: 1) they will be restored to the land promised by the Lord, and 2) they will be restored to God through the Lord Jesus. The last seven years of this age, known as Daniel's 70th week, or the Tribulation (the end times), is focused directly on the repentance and restoration of Israel. Daniel 9:24 explicitly states this. All of eschatology is aimed toward this purpose of Israel's restoration, in which the land promises play a pivotal role.

(If you would like to know more about end times events, you can reference my book *'The Time of the End: Unserstanding End Time Events'*, available on Amazon.)

*As a side note to the above Scripture, Galatians 3:28: while we are all one in spiritual position, we remain distinct in function. A male does not relinquish the roles of husband or father. There were still slaves when Paul wrote this. Females remain wives and mothers. Paul is not advocating for the relinquishing of our distinct, God-given responsibilities or roles. If we apply this in a functional sense, then there is no need for instruction to husbands and wives, as those roles would not exist. In a functional sense, this would mean there is no need for the fivefold ministry gifts in Ephesians 4:11, yet we see instruction to pastors and elders within the New Testament. This Scripture is also not advocating transgenderism or replacement theology. This Scripture is pointing out the greater reality that while we have certain functions, the confidence we have toward God is not found in those functions but rather in Christ. It is also pointing us to the truth of our equal position in the Lord, apart from our functions. Because our functions remain, this verse cannot be interpreted in a way that diminishes the role of the Jewish people. Being in Christ does not negate our natural functions or ethnicity.

Chapter Seven:

Not All Israel

One of the goals of this book is to look at Scripture that is used to bolster anti-Jew and anti-Israel sentiment. Romans 9:6 has gained notoriety lately due to a prominent Christian celebrity responding on his podcast to an exchange in an interview between a United States senator and a prominent media personality regarding Israel. What does that verse say, and how is it used to downplay Israel and the Jews? Romans 9:6 says, *"Not as though the word of God hath taken none effect. For they are not all Israel, which are of Israel"* (KJV). This verse, out of context, is used to show that not all the people in Israel, or from Israel, are really Israel. It is used to argue that the modern state of Israel is not biblical Israel. It is used to argue that the Jews are no longer "true" Israel. It is used to argue that those now in Israel are not genetically linked to the land but are actually "white European settlers" (or occupiers, depending on which group of people is speaking). But is that what this text is saying?

This text is speaking about who is descended ethnically from Israel. In this case, "Israel" is referring to Abraham, not Jacob or the nation. First, let's look at this passage from the translation that is quoted predominantly in this book, the Modern English Version: *"…For they are not all Israel who are* ***descended*** *from Israel."* There are many translations that render this verse this way. Now, at first glance, it appears that it could be saying that just because you are ethnically tied to Israel does not make you Israel. There are many who argue that the Jews are no longer considered "Israel." We will discuss that more in another chapter. But we must look at the context of this Scripture, as with any other Scripture. From Romans 9 through Romans 11, the Apostle Paul makes the argument that God can choose Gentiles because of His election. But he ends that argument in Romans 11 with this about Israel:

- "God has not rejected His people" (verses 1-2)
- "God can graft them back in" (verse 23)
- "All Israel will be saved" (verses 25-26)
- "As regarding **election**, they are beloved for the sake of the fathers" (verse 28)
- "The gifts and callings of God are irrevocable" (verse 29)

The Apostle Paul is speaking about those who are Abraham's physical descendants. Romans 9:6 is included in this context. In fact, in Romans 9:2–3, Paul states that his heart is heavy for his *"kinsmen according to the* ***flesh****."* In other words, his fellow Jews, not "spiritual Jews," but physical, ethnic Jews. Considering this context, Romans 9:6 cannot be saying that Jews are not Israel.

Verses 7–8 hold the key to this Scripture: *"and not all are children of Abraham because they are his offspring, but '****Through Isaac*** *shall your offspring be named.' This means that it is not the children of the flesh who are the children of God, but the children of the promise are counted as offspring."* Again, people will teach that the Jews are the children of the flesh, and Christians are the children of promise. It is true that Christians are considered "children of promise" (Galatians 3:26–29; 4:28). But this passage in Romans 9 is not speaking of the "children of faith," but of the descendants of Abraham *"through Isaac."*

Romans 9:9 solidifies this and tells us exactly to whom "children of promise" is referring: *"For this is what* ***the promise*** *said: 'About this time next year I will return, and* ***Sarah*** *shall have a son.'"* So, when the Apostle Paul says that "not all who are descended from Israel are Israel" in verse 6, he is saying that not all the **physical** descendants of Abraham can claim the blessing of Abraham. In other words, Ishmael is not Israel just because he descends from Abraham. Abraham married a woman named Keturah in Genesis 25; Keturah bore Abraham six more sons. They cannot claim the blessing of Abraham just because they are descended from Abraham. Romans 9:6 mentions descendants of Israel, but verse 7 identifies "Israel" in this case as Abraham. How is that so, if Jacob has historically and biblically always been called Israel?

Abraham As Israel

To answer that, we must look at a concept found in Hebrews 7. In this section of Scripture, the author of Hebrews speaks of Abraham paying tithes to Melchizedek, the high priest of God and king of Salem. He then mentions how Levi, the priests, receives tithes from people according to the law. Then he says something interesting in verses 9–10: *"One might say that Levi also, who receives tithes, paid tithes* ***through Abraham****, for he was* ***still in the loins*** *of his father when Melchizedek met Abraham."* In God's view, Levi paid tithes in Abraham because Levi was *"still in the loins."* In other words, the Levites were credited with paying tithes because their forefather paid tithes. Notice this verse mentions Abraham, not Jacob, as the father of the Levites. The Levites were a tribe that descended from Jacob's son Levi. Jacob was the patriarch renamed Israel by God. Yet Levi is said to have paid tithes in **Abraham**.

Why can the Apostle Paul call Abraham "Israel" in Romans 9:6–7? Because Isaac and Jacob, from whom Israel descended, came from the loins of Abraham. This is an ancient view of lineage and a spiritual principle as well.

In Romans 9, the Apostle Paul is making the larger argument that the descendants to whom the promises of the blessing of Abraham belong are from the line of Isaac and, ultimately, Jacob. Romans 9:4 in this context says, *"who are* ***Israelites, to whom belong*** *the adoption, the glory,* ***the covenants****, the giving of the law, the service of God, and* ***the promises****."* There is a reason that throughout Scripture, the Lord is called *"the God of Abraham, Isaac, and Jacob."* This is the absolute perspective of election: God chooses to whom the promises belong. He chose Abraham, Isaac, and Jacob. He is not bound to the traditions or laws of men.

Bless Those and Curse Those

As we look at this notion that "not all Israel is Israel," we should also look at another trope that has become popular in modern culture: that the Lord did not include Israel in the blessing to Abraham of *"bless those who bless you, and curse those who curse you."* This is a very popular topic among those who would dismiss Israel and the Jews as still having the Abrahamic Covenant. The first time this appears in Scripture is Genesis 12:3. The Lord is speaking to Abram (Abraham) as an individual.

In the previous section, we discussed the concept of Abraham as Israel and the ancient view of lineage. On that concept alone, we could make the argument that Israel carries that same blessing, as the descendants of promise, as being from the loins of Abraham. We also read of the same blessing spoken by Isaac to Jacob in Genesis 27:29. In ancient times, covenants passed from father to son. For the sake of argument, let's not consider these principles. We will set those aside for now, since they are spoken to individuals. So, then we must ask: is there anywhere in Scripture that the twelve tribes of Israel ever received that promise?

That brings us to Numbers 22–24. We read the account of the Israelites traveling to the plains of Moab in Numbers 22. The Moabites were terrified of them (verse 3). The king of the Moabites, Balak, hired the prophet Balaam to curse Israel. In Numbers 23, we read that instead of cursing Israel, Balaam spoke a blessing over them, as the Lord commanded him. Balak tries a different approach and attempts to convince Balaam to go through with cursing Israel. Again, Balaam spoke a blessing, as the Lord commanded. Balak asks him a third time to curse Israel. We pick up what Balaam speaks over Israel in chapter 24. Verses 2–3 say, *"When Balaam looked out and saw* ***Israel*** *encamped tribe by tribe,* ***the Spirit of God came on him*** *and he spoke his message…"* So now we see the Spirit of God comes on Balaam. So, these words are directly from the Lord! Balaam speaks a blessing over Israel and ends in verse 9a with this: *"May those who bless you be blessed and those who curse you be cursed!"*

This was spoken to the entire nation of Israel. It is in the context of this account that we see the Scripture we looked at previously, Numbers 23:19: *"God is not human, that he should lie, not a human being, that he should change his mind. Does he speak and then not act? Does he promise and not fulfill?"* The character of God's faithfulness is revealed in the *"bless those who bless you and curse those who curse you."* So, not only does Israel carry the same reciprocal prophecy of blessing and cursing of the everlasting covenant, but it is also guaranteed through God's faithfulness.

Some will say, "Jesus redeemed us from curses." Jesus redeemed us from the curse of the law (Galatians 3:13), not every curse. In fact, the book of Galatians goes on to say that we reap what we sow, which can be destruction or life (Galatians 6:7–8). We are free from the results of the curse of the **law**; we are saved from wrath and the judgment of sin (Romans 5:9; 1 Thessalonians 5:9; 1 John 2:1–2). We are not exempt from consequences.

The Apostle Paul gives a warning to Gentile believers about attitudes toward Jews in Romans 11. He warns them not to be arrogant toward them, not to be proud, but to fear, or a person can be cut off, or removed, just as the Jews were in their unbelief. We do not have the space here to go into a deep theological discussion of the concepts of being cut off or being cursed. What I will say is this: there is not enough fear of the Lord in this issue. I do not mean fear as in being afraid or terrified. I mean fear in its original sense: a reverential awe of the Lord and of His plans and purposes. When we consider the fear of the Lord from that perspective, it will negate a lot of arrogance.

CHAPTER EIGHT:

ENGRAFTMENT THEOLOGY

There are some very erroneous doctrines in the body of Christ concerning Israel and, by extension, the Jewish people. We will look at what these theologies teach and whether they hold up under scriptural scrutiny. We will discuss the more prominent theologies.

For the most part, these teachings seem to have the intent to honor the Lord, the Word, and His finished work. But in haste, and by not interpreting Scripture with Scripture, they have misinterpreted and misapplied the Scriptures. This is called proof-texting and eisegesis: making the Scriptures fit a bias by pulling the text out of context or, as one author describes it, "imposing a grid external to it."[1] Imposing an external grid over Scripture distorts what the text clearly says and conveys. There cannot be mental gymnastics to reach conclusions, or we end up doing what the Apostle Paul warns Timothy and Titus about concerning sound doctrine: "not giving heed to fables and myths...." (1 Tim. 1:3-4; Titus 1:14)

Replacement Theology

The first of these theologies, and the most prominent, is called "replacement theology" or "supersessionism." This theology teaches that the church has replaced Israel in God's plans and typically leads to the conclusion that the Jews have been rejected by God because they refused and killed their Messiah. The conclusion is that the church is now the "true Israel of God," or "spiritual Israel." (We discussed the Jews' rejection in **Chapter Four**.) It also states that all the blessings of Israel have been taken from the Jewish people and transferred to the church; this makes the land promises null and void. One author summed it up this way: "All the biblical statements of Israel enjoying future blessings in the land of Canaan are said to be descriptions of the spiritual blessings that now accrue to the church. The expectation of a physical kingdom has been spiritualized and taken from Israel and given to the Gentiles (the church)."[2] This theology ignores or denies most of the prophets, or it imposes an external grid of the church onto promises made to ethnic Israelites.

We must interpret Scripture based on the audience being addressed. In the case of the prophets, the intended audience was literal Israel. The theological error made by this imposition is that it requires shifting prophetic and eschatological focus to the church and excluding Israel. At no point in Scripture do we read of any such shift; coming to that conclusion requires reading into the text what it is not saying. What we do see is Jesus telling Jerusalem that *"…the kingdom of God will be taken from you and given to a nation bearing its fruits."* (Matthew 21:43) But after the resurrection, we read the disciples asking Jesus if He will restore the kingdom to Israel at that time. His answer? Not yet (Acts 1:6). This implies the kingdom will be restored to Israel, and the bigger takeaway for us is that God is not done with Israel. As the Apostle

Paul wrote in Romans 11:25: *"....a partial hardening has come upon Israel until the fullness of the Gentiles has come in".* In other words, it is only temporary.

When addressing replacement theology, we must look at one of the core New Testament verses used to defend this belief, Galatians 3:16. It seems that replacement theology hangs on this one verse, for the most part. This is what Galatians 3:16 states: *"Now the promises were made to Abraham and his Seed. He does not say, 'and to seeds,' meaning many, but 'and to your Seed,' meaning one, who is Christ."* The argument goes like this: all of God's promises in the Old Testament were not given to Israel but to Jesus. Since we are Abraham's seed through Christ (Galatians 3:29), then all of Israel's promises belong only to the church. Since Israel rejected Jesus, they are excluded from any covenant with God.

In context, is this what this verse is saying? When interpreting Scripture, we must ask: Why is the text being written? What is the underlying issue being addressed? In Galatians, Paul is addressing a *"different gospel"* (Galatians 1:6). What was this *"different gospel"*?

In Chapter 2, Paul talks about how Peter and Titus are affected by certain men: *"...false brothers were secretly brought in, who sneaked in to spy out our liberty, which we have in Christ Jesus, that they might bring us into bondage."* (verse 4) These men were called "Judaizers." They went behind Paul to the Gentiles, trying to persuade them to be circumcised and to follow the law of Moses. This matter was finally addressed in Acts 15. One of the teachings of Judaizers was to present circumcision as necessary for the blessings of Abraham. It is in this context that we reach Galatians 3. Paul begins to assure the Galatians that they received the Spirit through faith (verse 2); miracles come by the Spirit, not the law (verse 5); and he ends with this exhortation in verse 7: *"Therefore know that those who are of faith are the sons of Abraham."* Galatians 3 is not establishing the doctrine of replacement theology; it is Paul reassuring the Galatians that they are children of Abraham through faith in Christ, not the keeping of the law.

Verse 8 then tells us how the Scriptures (Hebrew Bible) foresaw that God would justify Gentiles. How did the Scripture record what was foreseen? *"And the Scripture, foreseeing that God would justify the Gentiles by faith, preached the gospel in advance to Abraham, saying,* ***"In you shall all the nations be blessed."*** That is the context of everything Paul is presenting leading up to verse 16. Verse 16 is a direct reference to Genesis 22:18. In the Abrahamic Covenant, it is the only place where "seed" is used as a singular. In every other instance in Genesis and the Abrahamic Covenant, the word "seed" is used as a **collective singular**, which would refer to descendants, offspring, or nation. So, when the Apostle Paul mentions *"seed" as "one"* in verse 16, he is saying that Christ fulfilled the promise of *"in you shall all the nations be blessed."* He is not saying that those in Christ have replaced Israel regarding the promises, especially the land promises. He goes on after verse 8 to explain further that Christ redeemed us from the curse of the law so that Abraham's blessing would come on the Gentiles **by faith** (verses 13–14). He concludes in verses 26–29 that they are sons of God by faith, and Abraham's descendants through faith.

In summary, Paul is rebuking the Galatians for following works and neglecting faith. He is making the argument that Christ redeemed them from the law and that their righteousness is not of circumcision or any other external show. Another Scripture that affirms this is Romans 2:26–29: *"Therefore, if an uncircumcised man keeps the righteousness of the law, will not his uncircumcision be counted as circumcision? Will the uncircumcised one who is righteous by nature, if he fulfills the law, not judge you who, by the letter of the law and circumcision, violate the law? He is not a Jew who is one outwardly, nor is circumcision that which is external in the flesh. But he is a Jew who is one inwardly. And circumcision is of the heart, by the Spirit, and not by the letter. His praise is not from men, but from God."* (This is another Scripture used to argue for replacement theology.) The Apostle Paul is not teaching replacement theology in either Romans 2 or Galatians 3; he is teaching righteousness by faith in Christ.

He is telling the Romans that righteousness is not based on external works (circumcision). He is reassuring the Galatians that their confidence should be in the finished work of Jesus, and that they should move away from *"a different gospel"*; that they are qualified for the blessing of Abraham through faith, not works. Is the church "spiritual Israel"? Yes, but that does not equal replacing ethnic Israel in God's plan, nor does it disqualify them from prophetic and eschatological fulfillment of the promises. Replacement theology overlooks Romans 9:3-4: *"For I could wish that I myself were accursed from Christ for my brothers,* ***my kinsmen by race, who are Israelites, to whom belong*** *the adoption, the glory, the covenants, the giving of the law, the service of God, and the promises."* These things belong to Israel by the election of God.

Fulfillment Theology

Fulfillment theology is sometimes confused with replacement theology. In many ways, it is a watered-down version of replacement theology. It recognizes the importance of Israel in God's plan but comes to the same conclusion as replacement theology: that God is finished with natural Israel. The reasoning is that since Jesus fulfilled the law, then all the promises have been fulfilled. I have heard proponents of this teaching say it this way: Jesus fulfilled the Old Testament.

Jesus Himself, in Matthew 5:17, said He fulfilled the law and the prophets (the Messianic prophecies). We saw in the previous section that Jesus fulfilled the portion of the Abrahamic Covenant that stated, *"in your seed shall all the families of the earth be blessed"* (Genesis 22:18; Galatians 3:16). But the Old Testament is not just the law and the Messianic prophecies. The one thing this teaching ignores is all the land promises in the **everlasting** covenant. It also ignores God's promises to draw Israel back into the land God promised to them through Abraham, Isaac, and Jacob.

Those have not been fulfilled yet; rather, Christ makes them sure (2 Corinthians 1:20). A promise being *"yes and amen"* does not mean it has happened, but rather that the means, or the legal instruments, necessary to guarantee the promise have been executed. In modern legal terms, a last will and testament does not confer immediate inheritance to the beneficiaries of that legal document, but it does guarantee it will be fulfilled. Israel's iniquities have been forgiven, the same as ours, by the same blood (Jeremiah 31:31-34; Hebrews 8:8-12; Hebrews 10:16-18). Jesus fulfilling the law and the prophets does not diminish the promises of restoration and repentance for Israel. We have already seen this principle in Galatians 3:17: one covenant does not annul another covenant. The law covenant was not abolished, but it was fulfilled. That very fulfillment makes the restoration of the kingdom to Israel guaranteed. It makes the repentance of Israel guaranteed as prophesied as well.

Ultimately, fulfillment theology makes the same error that replacement theology does in that it rejects the Jews and Israel as still having a covenant relationship with God. While replacement theology is very hostile toward the Jewish people, fulfillment theology is a bit softer in that regard. In my opinion, fulfillment theology is closer to the truth than replacement theology. It just falls short of the consummation of Jesus' fulfillment: God honoring the covenant given to Abraham, Isaac, and Jacob and their descendants, which will be fulfilled (restored) at His coming.

Dual Covenant Theology

When a believer defends Israel, they are often accused of holding to "dual covenant theology." Dual covenant theology teaches that the Mosaic law remains valid for salvation for the Jewish people, while Gentiles are saved through the New Covenant. For adherents to this theology, it is almost as if the Jews have a special means of salvation. I want to be clear: I do not advocate dual covenant theology. There is only one name under heaven by which any person can be saved, and that name is Jesus (Yeshua) (Acts 4:12). Jewish theologian David Stern, writing in the *Jewish New Testament'*, interprets Romans 10:4 as, *"For the goal at which the Torah aims is the Messiah, who offers righteousness to everyone who trusts."* [3] If the goal of the Torah is Jesus (Yeshua), then there is no special or separate plan of salvation for Israel. What Israel does have are the land promises in the Abrahamic covenant and the prophets' declarations of restoration and repentance.

Romans 10:12 tells us explicitly that there is no difference between the Jew and the non-Jew regarding salvation. Restoration and repentance, as we discussed previously in **Chapter 5**, are directly tied to Daniel's 70th week (the tribulation) and the coming of the Lord. There will be a mass revival of Israelites during that time, as prophesied in Zechariah 12:10, Romans 11:26-27, and Revelation 7:4-10. Regarding election, they are beloved because of the patriarchs (Abraham, Isaac, and

Jacob) (Romans 11:28). But they still must call on the name of the Lord for salvation (Acts 2:21; Acts 4:12; Romans 10:13).

Engraftment Theology

Considering these different theologies regarding Israel and the Jewish people, I would like to offer what I believe the Bible teaches about the mystery of Israel and the church. I have coined it "engraftment theology." This viewpoint is based on the Apostle Paul's discourse in Romans 9–11, the context of which is the salvation of the Jewish people. Paul describes what is happening spiritually between Jews and Gentiles. In Romans 9:30–31, Paul states that the Gentiles have attained righteousness by faith, but Israel has not attained it. He explains why in Romans 10:2–3: they have a zeal for God but are ignorant of God's righteousness. Paul then plainly tells us that God has not rejected Israel (Romans 11:1–2). They have been blinded, which we have discussed is temporary (Romans 11:25). In verse 17 of Chapter 11, Paul says, *"But if some of the branches were broken off, and you, being a wild olive shoot, were* ***grafted in*** *among them and became a partaker with them of the root and richness of the olive tree."* Paul is telling Gentiles (verse 13) that they have been *"grafted in"* to the olive tree. The olive tree is Israel.

That is why I call this "engraftment theology." We do not replace Israel; we are grafted into Israel; we enlarge Israel and become heirs with them. Romans 15:27 says that Gentiles **share** in the spiritual blessings of the Jewish people; we do not replace them. Romans 11:23–24 tells us that they can be grafted in again. Replacement theology would have us believe that God has utterly rejected the Jewish people, but that is simply not the case. Fulfillment theology is kinder in that it affirms that anyone can be saved (grafted in) by faith in Jesus, yet it still teaches that God's covenant relationship with Israel as a nation is over, having been fulfilled in Jesus. We will address that more in the next chapter, but for now, it is enough to say that this is a limited view.

Another post-resurrection (New Covenant) passage that supports engraftment theology is Ephesians 2:11–13: *"Therefore remember that formerly you, the Gentiles in the flesh, who are called the "uncircumcision" by the so-called "circumcision" in the flesh by human hands, were at that time apart from Christ,* **alienated from the citizenship of Israel and strangers to the covenants of promise**, *without hope and without God in the world. But now in Christ Jesus you who were formerly far away* **have been brought near** *by the blood of Christ."*

Apostle Paul plainly states that Gentiles were once alienated but have now been brought near by the blood of Jesus. Alienated from what, and brought near to what? To everything listed in those verses: the citizenship of Israel, the covenants of promise, hope, and God. Why would Paul mention the *"citizenship of Israel"*? Because we have been grafted into Israel by faith. We are descendants of Abraham by faith. But as Paul states in Romans 11:18, we cannot boast against the branches. This inclusion into the *"commonwealth of Israel"* (KJV) should soften our hearts toward the Jewish people. Why? Because we are partakers with them in the covenants of promise. Ephesians 2:19 states that we are now *"fellow citizens"* with them.

When we oppose them, we are working against God's purposes and plans. His purposes and plans are for them to be grafted in again to the olive tree. His purposes and plans, as we will see, include Jesus ruling from Jerusalem. This, in summary, is engraftment theology: Gentiles have been included as spiritual participants in God's blessing to Israel, but they have not replaced them.

We will end this chapter with Paul's warning to the Gentiles in Rome in Romans 11:18–22: *"Do not boast against the branches. If you boast, remember you do not sustain the root, but the root sustains you. You will say then, "The branches were broken off, so that I might be grafted in." This is correct. They were broken off because of unbelief, but you stand by faith. Do not be arrogant, but fear. For if God did not spare the natural branches, neither will He spare you. Therefore consider the goodness and severity of God—severity toward those who fell, but goodness toward you, if you continue in His goodness. Otherwise, you also will be cut off."*

CHAPTER NINE:

THE SPIRIT OF ANTICHRIST

The Bible tells us repeatedly that there is a spirit of antichrist in the world. This is not to be confused with the *"son of perdition"* that the Scriptures tell us about (2 Thessalonians 2:3, 8). This is a man we have called 'the antichrist'. The 'spirit of antichrist' is not the same thing as the man known as **the** antichrist. Many times, there is a conflation between the antichrist and the spirit of antichrist, but they are two separate entities. (Scriptures referring to the spirit of antichrist cannot be used in reference to the man called the antichrist.)

The antichrist (son of perdition; lawless one) is a man who leads the persecution of Israel in the Tribulation. The spirit of antichrist is the working of satan against God's plans, purposes, laws, precepts, and design. Things like homosexuality, transgenderism, and lawlessness are the work of the spirit of antichrist. The most notable feature of the spirit of antichrist is deception. Warnings against deception are throughout the Scriptures. The goal of the spirit of antichrist is twofold: 1) to bring people to a place of depravity and reprobate minds so that they do not see the truth of the gospel and the value of godliness. All vestiges of dignity and worth through God's precepts are replaced by moral relativism and human reasoning; and 2) to destroy the promises of God with the intent to overthrow God.

Regarding Israel, we have seen this throughout history. satan has worked to destroy Israel so he can destroy God's promise to them. Revelation 12:4 shows us this picture through John's vision on Patmos. Revelation 12:13 tells us that after the resurrection, satan *("the great dragon")* persecutes Israel. That is still happening today. The rebirth of Israel in 1948 did not stop him. If anything, his attacks against Israel intensified. Bearing witness to that are all the wars and intifadas against Israel from 1948 until now. The physical attacks notwithstanding, it is the propaganda surrounding Israel that is at the heart of deceiving the world. satan is the god of this world system and blinds their eyes (2 Corinthians 4:4). In my lifetime, I have not seen hatred for the Jewish people on the scale we are witnessing today. It is accelerated and magnified by social media. If you have ever wondered why *"the kings of the earth and their armies"* would ever *"surround Jerusalem,"* you are witnessing it in real time (Luke 21:20; Revelation 19:19). The endless rhetoric against the largest minority group in the world is amplified every day. In the next sections, we will look at a few of these deceptions.

The Synagogue of satan

This is a favorite trope of many on social media today. Any time the subject of Israel and the Jews is presented, there will inevitably be several people who put forward the idea that the Jewish people, and the nation of Israel, are the *"synagogue of satan"*. This idea comes from two Scriptures in Revelation 2:9 and 3:9. The gist of both verses is that there were Jews persecuting the churches being addressed (Smyrna and Philadelphia). He says these groups are the *"synagogue of satan"*. He identifies **those** Jews, not **all** Jews, as the synagogue of satan. Since the term "synagogue" is used, it is also possible that Jesus was referring to the leaders of those local Jewish communities, like what we discussed previously in **Chapter Four**.

Both passages in Revelation contain the phrase *"who say they are Jews but are not."* Some groups, which we will discuss a bit in the next chapter, have taken this to mean that the people who claim to be Jews today are not actually Jews. They have attached a conspiracy theory to this phrase and then try to apply it to modern-day Israel.

Jesus was quite possibly referring to the principle we see in Romans 2:28–29: a Jew is one inwardly, and circumcision is of the heart. Regarding salvation and submission to the Lord, claiming to be of the line of Abraham is not enough (John 3:7–9; John 8:39). Obedience is better than sacrifice (1 Samuel 15:22). Jesus calls the leaders of that day *"whitewashed tombs"* (Matthew 23:27–28). He also called the leaders of His day *"of your father, the devil"* (John 8:44). So, there is a strong possibility that this is the interpretation of that phrase.

In any case, to say all Jewish people are the *"synagogue of satan"* is not only a misrepresentation of Scripture, but it also dehumanizes the Jewish people. This leads to the justification of negative behavior and sentiment toward them. The Jewish people, and the nation of Israel, are not the "*synagogue of satan*". Calling all Jews the *"synagogue of satan"* is akin to saying that all Germans are Nazis. It is an intellectual and biblical fallacy.

The Star of Remphan

This is another favorite social media trope these days: equating the Star of David, which is used on Israel's national flag and has become a symbol of the Jewish people, to the *"star of Remphan"* mentioned in Acts 7:43. The insinuation is that Israel and the Jewish people worship a pagan god and are cultists. It is also used to bolster the conspiracy theory of being the *"synagogue of satan"*.

First, let me address the fact that images and symbols are just that. There are many ancient symbols used and repurposed throughout antiquity, including the pentagram and the swastika. That hardly links all cultures using those symbols as having the same intents and purposes. The Star of David was chosen for two reasons: 1) it was well known throughout Jewish communities around the world, going back as far as the 14th century and gaining widespread use in the 19th century;[1] and 2) it did not carry the religious significance that other symbols did.[1] Furthermore, the *"star of Remphan"* is an eight-pointed star, not six-pointed like the Star of David.[2]

Stephen's discourse in Acts 7:43 was not to bring attention to a "star," nor was he claiming that the audience he was addressing was worshipping idols. In fact, he speaks about the *"star of Remphan"* almost in passing, and most certainly in the context of a larger historical narrative. He is simply referring to the history of Israel, and he sums up his point in Acts 7:51: *"You stiff-necked people, uncircumcised in heart and ears! You always resist the Holy Spirit. As your fathers did, so do you.*" Making the Star of David a focal point is yet another conspiracy theory and is full of presumption and assumption. It presumes to know what the Star of David represents when history clearly shows what it means to the Jewish people. There is no historical record that King David ever used the symbol at all. It is from Jewish tradition, and the Jewish people have attached David's name to it because of the Messianic implications of the Davidic Covenant (2 Samuel 7:8–17; 1 Chronicles 17:11–14).

Every indication of the *"star of Remphan"* is that it was not actually the image of a star, but an idol made to represent a "star-god." It is linked to the worship of the planet Saturn.[2] Amos 5:26, which Acts 7:43 refers to, says this in the NRSV: *"You shall take up Sakkuth your king and Kaiwan your* ***star god****, your* ***images****,* ***which you made for yourselves****.*" An idol was used as a representation of the object to be worshipped. In this case, it was not a star, but a "star-god." That would indicate that the idol would look like a person, or possibly an animal, or a hybrid. We see these throughout antiquity.

The history of Israel clearly shows they had a propensity to be influenced by the peoples around them. Just a little over a month removed from Egypt in the Exodus, they pressured Aaron to build an idol of a golden calf (Exodus 32:1–4). This was the influence of Egypt on them. This was most likely the case that Amos and Stephen were referencing. The *"star of Remphan"* conspiracy theory does not hold biblical scrutiny. It is simply another slander of the Jewish people, and a means of social media content for creators.

Zionism and Anti-Zionism

The terms "Zionism," "Zionist," and "Christian Zionist" have taken on very derogatory connotations recently. The terms have been warped and are used in such a way as to try to create defensiveness in anyone who considers themselves pro-Israel. They are used to shame people into silence. It is very similar to the way race is used when discussing political ideals in our modern day. If someone has an opposing stance on a political ideal, they hurl a derogatory accusation of "racist" to put people on the defensive. It creates a need to try to prove you are not the thing they accuse you of being.

In America, if you support Israel, you are automatically branded as "Israel First" and against America; this is an intellectual fallacy. Two things can be true at the same time. I can simultaneously be pro-Israel and "America First." Some will go as far as to say you cannot follow Christ and support the Jews. All the shame and rhetoric from these people are rooted in a warped idea of what Zionism is.

In their worldview, Zionism is an attempt by the nation of Israel to rule the world. They see Israel, and by extension the Jewish people, as the cause of all the world's problems throughout history. They believe that Israel is controlling most of the governments of the world. But this view is not consistent with historical Zionism. Historically, Zionism is simply the belief that the Jewish people have a right to self-determination in their ancestral homeland. When someone claims to be "anti-Zionist," they are denying that the Jewish people should have the right to self-determination. Zionism holds that the only way for the Jewish people to have self-determination is to be in their ancestral homeland. Of course, there are many who do not believe that the modern nation of Israel is their homeland. This belief imposes a secondary meaning onto Zionism as being a movement that takes land by force. We will discuss this more in the next chapter.

One thing you will notice with anti-Zionists is that they use language that does not simply deny the nation of Israel the right to exist; the rhetoric begins to devolve into pre-Holocaust language. There is a large segment of anti-Zionists who believe Hitler and the Nazis were right to try to exterminate the Jewish people. Some deny the Holocaust happened. This is the spirit of antichrist at work. How reprobate do you have to be to advocate for the extermination of an entire ethnic group? This is usually done as Israel is falsely accused of genocide of the Palestinian people in Gaza. Under this premise, the answer to genocide would be genocide. These same people claim to operate from truth.

Why push so vehemently for the destruction of the smallest minority in the world? Because the "great dragon" is waging war on Israel through the blinded eyes and hardened hearts of mankind, all while they claim illumination. Too often, anti-Zionism is the bridge to anti-Jew. Eventually, the two become conflated, and anti-Jew sentiment becomes absorbed into anti-Zionism for many. This plays exactly into the spirit of antichrist's aims.

They Hate Jesus

One justification that anti-Zionists will use is that the Jewish people, especially those who still practice Judaism, hate Jesus, going as far back as the trial and crucifixion of the Lord to further their narrative. Unfortunately, this is a major theological misunderstanding. In John 10:17-18, Jesus says, *"Therefore My Father loves Me, because I lay down My life that I may take it up again. No one takes it from Me, but I lay it down Myself. I have power to lay it down, and I have power to take it up again. I received this command from My Father."* Jesus laid down His life as He was commanded by the Father to do so.

Were the Jews used as the instrument of that, especially the Jewish leaders? Yes. Although the Romans carried out the crucifixion of Jesus, the Jewish leaders forced their hand. But if Christ had not died, then we would all still be in our sins.

Salvation, which is of the Jews (John 4:22), would not have been made available to the world (to the **Jew first**, then to the Greek, Romans 1:16). This was all done according to the will of God. He took our sin and we received His righteousness (2 Corinthians 5:21). This narrative against the Jews is a major theological oversight. It overlooks God's plan in man's redemption.

The people using this justification will look at modern Judaism as their proof of this, even saying that Muslims honor Jesus more than Jews. Muslims do not believe Jesus was the Son of God, only a prophet. This is more of the spirit of antichrist delusion.* It is true that Judaism doesn't recognize Jesus; blindness has happened in part to them (Romans 11:25). So, the premise is flawed. If we apply that same premise, then we must apply the same vitriol to Hindus, Sikhs, Buddhists, and so on. But does that happen? Of course not. Maybe it would be a good idea to share the gospel with the Jewish people, not out of arrogance or condescension, but out of love. The Jews may not recognize Jesus as the Messiah yet, but that does not equal "the Jews hate Jesus." So why differentiate them from others in that regard? Because the god of this world system has blinded their eyes (2 Corinthians 4:4).

Eschatological Implications

The spirit of antichrist is working to destroy the Jewish people and the nation of Israel to stop God's promise to the descendants of Abraham through Isaac and Jacob. All of eschatology (end-time events) is aimed at Israel. The Scriptures declare that Jesus will descend to the Mount of Olives and reign over all the nations from Jerusalem (Zechariah 14; Jeremiah 3:17). satan has tried to destroy Jerusalem for centuries: first with the Babylonians (587

BC), then with the Romans (AD 70). Now, he is trying to wrest it out of the hands of the Jews. His goal is to stop the fulfillment of prophecy. It is his attempt to destroy God's Word and His promises. satan has always cast doubt on God's Word, trying to brand Him as untrustworthy. He did it in the Garden of Eden, and he does it now.

Make no mistake: it is the Word of God he is after, not you, not me, not the Jewish people. We are just in the way of his goals. Understanding the eschatological implications of the spirit of antichrist should turn our hearts toward the Jewish people. We should be praying for revival in Israel. We should be praying for Jewish people to receive their Messiah. After all, that is part of our gospel mission (Romans 10:19; Romans 11:11, 14).

Christians have taken the stance for centuries that since the Jews were dispersed from Israel by the Romans (AD 70 and AD 135), then God was finished with them, and any references to Israel were simply spiritual metaphors for the church. This completely ignores prophecy and the historical context of those prophecies. When Israel was reestablished in 1948, it should have been a wake-up call to believers. Unfortunately, most doubled down and labeled Israel's return as a nation a secular act brought about by world governments who felt guilty about the Holocaust. God can use secular people and governments to bring about His ends. He used Assyria and Babylon in judgment against Israel and Judah. In the same way, He used governments to reestablish Israel in fulfillment of His promises. It is time we wake up to prophecy unfolding before us.

*For more on this, see my book *The Time of the End: Understanding End-Time Events, available* on Amazon.

CHAPTER TEN:

POLITICS AND THE WORLD

The issue the world has with Israel stems from unbelief in the Word of God. They do not believe this covenant; therefore, they see the reinstatement of the nation of Israel as a Jewish state as illegitimate. They see it through the eyes of politics, which is part of the world system. They create conspiracy theories to justify their hatred of Jews. It is a historically illiterate view of that region and its people.

Contrary to mainstream political commentary, history shows that there has been a continuous Jewish presence in the land for 3,000 years. The land previously known as Canaan has only ever had one united kingdom within its borders, and that was Israel. In the days before the Israelite monarchy, the area was settled into city-states. After the fall of the northern and southern kingdoms, there was no single nation within its borders. The land was under the control of different empires until 1948. Babylonians, Greeks, Romans, Ottomans, and the British all ruled over this land until 1948.

There was never a nation known as Palestine. It was called Judea under Roman rule until after the revolt of Simon bar Kochba in AD 135. At that time, it was renamed Syria Palaestina, which later became Palestine. It referred to a region, not a nation. Even then, there was a Jewish presence. The designation "Palestinian" referred to anyone living in the region, including Jews, Muslims, and Christians. In 1964, Yasser Arafat insisted that the designation "Palestinian" be used only to refer to Arabs. The world went along with him, yet another deception by the spirit of antichrist.

Israel did not go in and steal land from the "Palestinians." The land was under British control. The British, working with the United Nations, established a two-state solution. The Arabs rejected the solution and immediately waged war against the newly formed state of Israel. Every time a solution of peace has been presented, the Arabs rejected it and Israel accepted it, every single time (1937, 1947, 1967, 1973, 2000, and 2008). Even when it was not to its advantage, Israel accepted the terms to attempt peace, but the Arabs did not.

The politics of the world ignore these historical facts. Israel is the only democratic state in the Middle East, which is another conveniently ignored fact. Jews, Christians, and Muslims all have representation within the government of Israel. Each group has equal standing as citizens, although certain social media commentators say otherwise.

Israel is not occupying "Palestine." Media pundits and politicians point to the use of checkpoints around Gaza and the West Bank as proof of occupation. The truth is that these are defensive measures put in place after the First and Second Intifadas (1987–1993; 2000–2005). These intifadas (Arabic for rebellion or uprising) were marked by a series of suicide bombings within Israel's borders. Checkpoints are used at Israel's borders to protect its citizens; it is self-preservation, not apartheid. "Occupation" is the terminology used because it invokes images of subjugation through military presence. It is evident that the politics of the world have sided with the Arab world, and by extension Islam, against Israel.

White European Colonizers

Another conspiracy theory that is popular these days is the notion that the Jews in the land today are not of Middle Eastern descent. The claim is that they are white European settlers who have co-opted Jewish identity in a quest for power. There are groups who try to trace genealogy and come up with the "Khazar theory." This theory, in a nutshell, posits that the Jews in Israel who resettled in 1948 were descended from Turkish converts to Judaism from the Caucasus region of Central and Eastern Asia. This claim has been debunked through genetic testing, linguistics, and archaeology.[1] It is used by those with anti-Jewish bias to delegitimize the Jewish presence in Israel. It is a belief rooted in conspiracy theory, with no historical or scientific foundation. But it does fit a narrative.

Unfortunately, human nature is such that instead of admitting wrong thinking and beliefs, people dig their feet in to protect their worth. It does not matter how much research one does if the basic premise is faulty. It simply means a person has accumulated a lot of faulty knowledge. Not to mention how much "research" is simply seeking confirmation bias.

The argument of "white Jews" basically stands on the premise that a person of Jewish (Middle Eastern) descent would have darker skin. This premise does not consider that Jewish people migrated across the world for centuries in the diaspora. Basic genetics teaches us that skin tone can change in as few as three generations, especially with intermarriage. In this case, approximately 65 generations were removed from their ancestral homeland. Climate adaptation alone could cause a skin tone change in that amount of time. Skin tone changes, but DNA does not. There is no DNA evidence that proves this conspiracy theory. On the contrary, there is plenty of evidence to disprove that theory. Making a claim that denies a person's Jewishness because of the color of their skin must be dismissed out of hand.

Genocide

The current falsehood making the mainstream rounds these days is that Israel is committing genocide in Gaza. Social media commentators present this as fact while giving no evidence. The entire narrative relies on "eyewitness accounts" of Palestinians who have been displaced because of the war on Hamas, and on the Ministry of Health in Gaza (which is run by Hamas). These are not exactly unbiased sources.

What is missing in these reports is context. First, let's not forget why this current conflict started. Hamas attacked Israel on October 7th, 2023, killing not only men but women, children, and babies, while also taking 251 hostages; of those 251 hostages, 85 were killed. Second, the Gazan Ministry of Health only reports numbers and includes Hamas combatants as civilians. Nor do they mention that Hamas hides in tunnels built under schools and hospitals and uses women and children as human shields. Not to mention that Israel warned civilians in Gaza, and Hamas prevented them from leaving. When this context is taken as a whole, there is not a genocide taking place.

Proponents of this narrative claim that Israel allowed Hamas to attack to give them a justification to commit genocide and take

Palestinian land. This is yet another baseless conspiracy theory that simply confirms anti-Israel bias. This narrative proposes that Israel wanted Gaza's land. This claim falls short historically. After the 1967 Six-Day War, which was initiated by the Arab world against Israel, the land under Israeli control included the Sinai Peninsula, the Golan Heights, the West Bank, and Gaza. The Sinai Peninsula was returned to Egypt in 1982. Israel fully withdrew from Gaza in 2005. They have not given up control of the Golan Heights and the West Bank.

If Israel wanted the land in Gaza, why did they withdraw in 2005? Why not keep it like the other territories under its control? This conflict is not about land; it is about Israel's self-preservation. Hamas has proven they will continue to attack Israel. What choice does Israel have?

From The River To The Sea

We have all heard the chant during pro-Palestinian (anti-Israeli) protests on college campuses and in streets around the world: "From the river to the sea, Palestine will be free!" This is a literal call for the eradication of the Jewish people. It extends beyond Israel and Gaza and is now being echoed against Jewish communities around the world. The message is clear: Israel doesn't have the right to exist as a self-determining nation, and Jews are no longer welcome anywhere. The only alternative in that scenario is the destruction of Jewish people. The persecution of the Jewish people is on full display and intensifying every day.

Although many news outlets, politicians, and commentators claim that Arabs and Muslims want peace with Israel, history does not support that assessment. In 1947, the Arab League was formed. Its initial goal, at least internally, was to prevent the establishment of an Israeli state. Once Israel was established in 1948, the stated goal shifted to the destruction of Israel. Groups such as ISIS, Hamas, Hezbollah, and the PLO have charters that call for Israel's destruction. That is a primary platform for these groups. Supposedly, the PLO changed its charter, but the original charter still exists on some Palestinian Authority websites.

These events foreshadow prophetic fulfillment. It is bad enough that the spirit of antichrist is working through bad actors against Israel, but many believers are taking up the cause against them as well. They claim to be "enlightened" about Israel, yet they are working hand in hand with the spirit of antichrist. Eventually, this will lead to a coalition of ten Arab nations working together to destroy Israel. In time, they will consolidate their power in the individual known as the "son of perdition" or "lawless one" (2 Thessalonians 2:3, 8).* These events will lead to the Great Tribulation.* We are witnessing the lead-up to end-times prophecy. "From the river to the sea" will be the chant that ultimately unites the world against Israel.

World Control

Another favorite narrative among political pundits and social media commentators is that Israel and the Jews control the world. All the governments of the world are supposedly in the pocket of Israel. Here in America, any politician who expresses support for Israel is called a puppet. Then there is the narrative that all the industries of the world are controlled by Jewish elites. These narratives can be traced as far back as the thirteenth century. It is nothing new, but the modern narrative, considering geopolitical issues today, creates suspicion of Jewish people and leads to discriminatory actions against them, including violence.

There are Jewish people who are wealthy and powerful, and some possibly have bad intentions. But that does not equal "the Jews/Israel control the world." If the Jews/Israel controlled the world as suggested (politics, banking, media), you would never hear any negative commentary from any politician or media pundit.

Anyone who watches television or listens to podcasts can tell you that is not the case. In banking, funding could be cut off to any group that opposes Israel. That does not happen. Media outlets that do not support Israel would be shut down. Again, that is not happening. The very nature of Israel's strategic partnerships with other countries shows the opposite of world control. These are reciprocal relationships, especially the U.S.-Israel alliance. Aid sent to Israel is different from aid sent to other countries. The U.S. receives technology and military benefits from Israel that are not received from any other country. Another entire book could be written on this topic alone. For some insight, here is a fact about the strategic partnership between the two countries: "The economic relations between the United States and Israel generate yearly $50 billion worth of bilateral trade that supports a job market of 255,000 Americans."[2] This does not sound like a country or people who want to dominate the world.

CONCLUSION

The historical fact remains that Israel and the Jewish people are among the most maligned in world history. The conspiracy theories aimed at them can make your head spin. We know the source of this is the spirit of antichrist. It will not get better. Biblical prophecy declares it will get worse. Jewish persecution will escalate, leading to what the prophet Jeremiah calls *"the time of Jacob's trouble"* (Jeremiah 30:7). This is repeated and rephrased in Daniel and Matthew as *"a time of trouble (great tribulation) such as never* has been *since there was a nation…"* (Daniel 12:1; Matthew 24:21).

In the meantime, believers should stand with the Jewish people and pray for them. Does that mean the nation of Israel is above reproach? Not at all. But we must be careful to separate truth from false narratives. When the Lord told Abraham and Israel, *"I will curse those who curse you,"* the word used for *"curse"* can also carry the sense of slander. You do not have to actively participate in persecution to be guilty; if you slander or bear false witness, you are guilty of cursing Israel and the Jewish people.

Ultimately, Scripture tells us that the Lord Jesus will come to the defense of the Jewish people, and they will accept their Messiah. Until then: **AmYisraelChai!** (The people of Israel live!)

*For more on this, see my book *The Time of the End: Understanding End-Time Events, available* on Amazon.

About the Author

Randall Rittenberry lives in Cookeville, Tennessee with his wife, Cynthia. He has two children, and four grandchildren. Since 1995, he has served as a counselor, pastor, and teacher. He has served in, and developed, ministries within the local church including: helps (ushers and greeters), children's ministry, youth ministry, and worship. He has held leadership and administrative positions in churches, including being an associate pastor and senior pastor, and a national ministerial organization. Randall holds a degree in theology from Impact Int'l School of Ministry. He has a passion to help people develop to their full potential, become disciples of Jesus, and to see themselves the way God sees them. For more info go to:

www.randallrittenberry.com

You can find teaching resources there such as videos, podcasts, and articles.

Other books by this author:

Discovering Purpose

Finding God's Plan For Your Life

Psalm 19:14 Setting Your Heart

Scriptures To Renew Your Mind and Establish Your Heart

Breaking Free

Overcoming Depression Through Biblical Principles

The Time of the End

Understanding End Time Events

These can be found on Amazon or at the author's website:

www.randallrittenberry.com

BIBLIOGRAPHY

Preface

1.https://www.reuters.com/world/americas/antisemitic-anti-israeli-attacks-around-world-since-october-7-2023-2025-10-02/

https://apnews.com/article/israel-antisemitism-report-australia-tel-aviv-hamas-gaza-239c233a7b2e08b3cc1659866eba4b59

2.https://www.usnews.com/news/world-report/articles/2024-10-07/report-antisemitic-incidents-reach-record-high-in-year-since-oct-7-attack

https://www.timesofisrael.com/us-antisemitism-up-337-since-october-7-in-all-time-record-adl-says/

https://www.mideastjournal.org/post/antisemitism-since-oct-7-surges-worldwide

https://thehill.com/blogs/blog-briefing-room/4646435-antisemitism-surging-worldwide-since-october-7-attack-report/

https://www.nbcnews.com/news/us-news/antisemitic-incidents-us-jumped-360-oct-7-hamas-attack-advocacy-group-rcna133104

https://www.independent.co.uk/news/world/americas/october-7-antisemitism-attacks-us-b2625190.html

3. https://momentmag.com/antisemitism-monitor-2025/

4. https://www.newadvent.org/fathers/0128.htm

Chapter 1

1. Ezekiel 5:5

2. Genesis 17:21 "But I will establish My covenant with Isaac, whom Sarah will bear to you at this set time next year."

Chapter 3

1. https://www.differentspirit.org/resources/land.php

2. Gnosticism has many variations, but the main characteristic of any form of Gnosticism is the belief that one carries secret knowledge or understands a higher form of knowledge than others. Typically, for others to gain this secret knowledge for themselves requires them to seek out and learn from someone who has this knowledge.

3. Genesis 15:9-18

Chapter 4

1. Isaiah 40:1-3 "Comfort, comfort My people, says your God. Speak tenderly to the heart of Jerusalem, and cry to her that her time of service and her warfare are ended, that [her punishment is accepted and] her iniquity is pardoned, that she has received [punishment] from the Lord's hand double for all her sins. A voice of one who cries: Prepare in the wilderness the way of the Lord [clear away the obstacles]; make straight and smooth in the desert a highway for our God!"

Chapter 8

1. Robert Alter, *The Art of Biblical Narrative* (New York: Basic Books, 2011), x–xi.

2. Rev. Malcolm Hedding https://icejusa.org/replacement-theology/

3. David H. Stern, *Jewish New Testament*, Messianic Jewish Publishers, 2023.

Chapter 9

1.https://www.israelhayom.com/2024/10/31/the-contested-history-of-the-star-of-david/

2.https://www.douglashamp.com/remphan-is-ninurta-his-star-has-eight-points/

Chapter 10

1.https://www.adl.org/resources/article/untangling-false-claims-about-ashkenazi-jews-khazars-and-israel

https://forward.com/opinion/382967/ashkenazi-jews-are-not-khazars-heres-the-proof/

https://forward.com/fast-forward/381367/why-did-23andme-tell-ashkenazi-jews-they-could-be-descended-from-khazars/

2.https://brusselsmorning.com/why-does-the-us-support-israel-historical-strategic-and-economic-perspectives/73082/